KNOWN UNKNOWNS:
UNCONVENTIONAL "STRATEGIC SHOCKS" IN DEFENSE STRATEGY DEVELOPMENT

Nathan Freier

November 2008

The views expressed in this report are those of the author and do not necessarily reflect the official policy or position of the Department of the Army, the Department of Defense, or the U.S. Government. This report is cleared for public release; distribution is unlimited.

Comments pertaining to this report are invited and should be forwarded to: Director, Strategic Studies Institute, U.S. Army War College, 122 Forbes Ave, Carlisle, PA 17013-5244.

The author would like to thank the following individuals and organizations for their significant contributions to this work. First, I am grateful to my colleagues at the Center for Strategic and International Studies, particularly Sam Brannen, Kathleen Hicks, Clark Murdock, and Christine Wormuth. Our interaction over the summer was decisive in clarifying my thoughts. Next, I would like to thank Mr. D. Burgess Laird of the Institute for Defense Analysis for encouraging me to write this monograph in the first place and providing important advice at the front end of the project. I am also grateful to Dr. Phil Williams both of the University of Pittsburgh and the U.S. Army War College's Strategic Studies Institute. Dr. Williams' advice and precision editing were instrumental in the project's completion. I am further grateful for the contributions of Dr. Carl van Dyke of the National Intelligence Council. His input was instrumental in strengthening my final arguments. As always, I am also beholden to the other authors cited in this work. And, finally, this monograph would not have been possible without support from the U.S. Army War College's Peacekeeping and Stability Operations Institute. Their provision of a hospitable venue for research and writing made this work and future like works possible.

All Strategic Studies Institute (SSI) publications are available on the SSI homepage for electronic dissemination. Hard copies of this report also may be ordered from our homepage. SSI's homepage address is: *www.StrategicStudiesInstitute.army.mil.*

PKSOI's website address is *https://pksoi.army.mil.*

*****

The Strategic Studies Institute publishes a monthly e-mail newsletter to update the national security community on the research of our analysts, recent and forthcoming publications, and upcoming conferences sponsored by the Institute. Each newsletter also provides a strategic commentary by one of our research analysts. If you are interested in receiving this newsletter, please subscribe on our homepage at *www.StrategicStudiesInstitute.army.mil/newsletter/.*

FOREWORD

This timely PKSOI Paper on unconventional strategic shock provides the defense policy team a clear warning against excessive adherence to past defense and national security convention. Including the insights of a number of noted scholars on the subjects of "wild cards" and "strategic surprise," the author, Nathan Freier, argues that future disruptive, unconventional shocks are inevitable. Through strategic impact and potential for disruption and violence, defense-relevant unconventional shocks, in spite of their nonmilitary character, will demand the focused attention of defense leadership, as well as the decisive employment of defense capabilities in response. As a consequence, Mr. Freier makes a solid case for continued commitment by the Department of Defense to prudent strategic hedging against their potential occurrence.

The Peacekeeping and Stability Operations Institute and the Strategic Studies Institute are pleased to offer this insightful monograph as a contribution to the debate on this important national security issue.

JOHN A. KARDOS
Colonel, U.S. Army
Director
Peacekeeping and Stability
Operations Institute

DOUGLAS C. LOVELACE, JR.
Director
Strategic Studies Institute

BIOGRAPHICAL SKETCH OF THE AUTHOR

NATHAN FREIER is a Visiting Professor of Strategy, Policy, and Risk Assessment at the U.S. Army's Peacekeeping and Stability Operations Institute and a Senior Fellow in the International Security Program at the Center for Strategic and International Studies (CSIS). Mr. Freier joined CSIS in April 2008 after retiring from the U.S. Army after 20 years as a lieutenant colonel. His last military assignment was as Director of National Security Affairs at the U.S. Army War College's Strategic Studies Institute. Prior to that, he served in the Office of the Deputy Assistant Secretary of Defense for Strategy, where his principal responsibilities included development of the 2005 National Defense Strategy. Previously, he was an Army fellow/visiting scholar at the University of Maryland's Center for International and Security Studies and a strategist with the Strategy, Plans, Concepts, and Doctrine Directorate, Department of the Army Staff in Washington, DC. Mr. Freier twice deployed to Iraq as a strategist while assigned to the Army War College. From January to July 2005, he served in the Strategy, Plans, and Assessments Directorate of Headquarters, Multi-National Force–Iraq, and from May to August 2007, he served as a special assistant to the Commander, Multi-National Corps–Iraq, in the Commander's Initiatives Group. In his current capacity, he continues to provide expert advice to a number of key actors in the security and defense policymaking and analysis communities. Among his research interests and areas of expertise are U.S. grand strategy; national security, defense, and military strategy and policy development; irregular, catastrophic, and hybrid security challenges and conflicts; strategic net and risk assessment; terrorism; and the Iraq War. Mr. Freier holds masters' degrees in International Relations from Troy State University and Politics from The Catholic University of America.

SUMMARY

The current defense team confronted a game-changing "strategic shock" in its first 8 months in office. The next team would be well-advised to expect the same. Defense-relevant strategic shocks jolt convention to such an extent that they force sudden, unanticipated change in the Department of Defense's (DoD) perceptions about threat, vulnerability, and strategic response. Their unanticipated onset forces the entire defense enterprise to reorient and restructure institutions, employ capabilities in unexpected ways, and confront challenges that are fundamentally different than those routinely considered in defense calculations.

The likeliest and most dangerous future shocks will be unconventional. They will not emerge from thunderbolt advances in an opponent's military capabilities. Rather, they will manifest themselves in ways far outside established defense convention. Most will be nonmilitary in origin and character, and not, by definition, defense-specific events conducive to the conventional employment of the DoD enterprise.

They will rise from an analytical no man's land separating well-considered, stock and trade defense contingencies and pure defense speculation. Their origin is most likely to be in irregular, catastrophic, and hybrid threats of "purpose" (emerging from hostile design) or threats of "context" (emerging in the absence of hostile purpose or design). Of the two, the latter is both the least understood and the most dangerous.

Thoughtful evaluation of defense-relevant strategic shocks and their deliberate integration into DoD strategy and planning is a key check against excessive convention. Further, it underwrites DoD relevance and resilience. Prior anticipation of September 11, 2001 (9/11) or the Iraq insurgency, for example, might have limited the scope and impact of the shock. In both instances, wrenching periods of post-event self-examination did help solve our current or last problem. They may not have been as effective in solving our next one.

DoD is now doing valuable work on strategic shocks. This work must endure and mature through the upcoming political transition. The next defense team should scan the myriad waypoints and end points along dangerous trend lines, as well as the prospect for sudden, discontinuous breaks in trends altogether to identify the next shock or shocks. Doing so is a prudent hedge against an uncertain and dangerous future.

KNOWN UNKNOWNS:[1]
UNCONVENTIONAL "STRATEGIC SHOCKS" IN DEFENSE STRATEGY DEVELOPMENT

INTRODUCTION: THE FAILURE OF IMAGINATION[2]

A thoughtful senior policy official has opined that most potentially devastating threats to U.S. interests start being evaluated as unlikely.

Jack Davis[3]

Defense analysis and strategy are inherently reactive. Historically, defense strategy development and planning have demonstrated three critical flaws. For too long, they have been *overly reactive.* Corporately, they have *lacked sufficient imagination.* And, as a result, both have been *vulnerable to surprise.*

Recent history indicates that defense strategy and planning fail to be sufficiently predictive. When they do venture into prediction, it often comes as linear extrapolation of contemporary challenges, adhering too closely to current convention. These are artifacts of defense conservatism, finite resources, and Bureaucracy 101.

Senior defense and military leadership naturally err on the side of what is known and practiced at the expense of preparing for what is less well-known but perhaps more dangerous. There is an inherent predilection against anything that smacks of speculation. This trend is natural and narrowly reasonable. Cautious senior leaders see too much at stake in the near-term to countenance instituting disruptive institutional change that is predicated on predictive analysis. In their view, there are enough compelling challenges in

1

the Department of Defense's (DoD) in-box to consume the focus of senior leaders and strategists. Yet, in the contemporary environment, focusing exclusively on the known, practiced, and narrowly reasonable is also naïve. At this juncture, engaging in some sound speculation is increasingly prudent.

Like the attacks of September 11, 2001 (9/11), the subsequent War on Terrorism (WoT), and the Iraq insurgency, the next defense-relevant challenge is likely to be a strategically dislocating surprise.[4] Without continued and more sophisticated "horizon scanning," there is near-certainty that the next compelling *defense-relevant* challenge will be a "strategic shock."[5] The current administration confronted a game-changing "strategic shock" inside its first 8 months in office. The next administration would be well-advised to expect the same during the course of its first term.[6]

Strategic shocks jolt convention to such an extent that they force affected institutions to fundamentally reorient strategy, strategic investments, and missions. DoD's post-9/11 adjustment to counterterrorism (CT) and counterinsurgency (COIN) illustrates this point. Some of DoD's reorientation on CT and COIN was prudent and necessary, but also, at the same time, late and reactive. Without comprehensive net and risk assessment of future shocks, any defense adjustment based on yesterday's experience but nonetheless intended for tomorrow's unconventional demands could prove far off the mark downstream.

Senior defense leaders and strategists have key questions to answer on the subject of strategic shocks. This monograph examines the role of the strategic shock in contemporary defense strategy development. It targets the incoming senior defense team, seeking to encourage them to institutionalize defense-relevant shocks in long-range defense strategy and planning efforts. It attempts to begin answering four important questions on the subject: (1) What are strategic shocks? (2) What obstacles militate against their routine employment in DoD strategy development? (3) Why are strategic shocks important to strategy and planning? And, finally, (4) What kinds of shocks would profoundly impact future DoD decisionmaking?

Meaningful consideration of shocks in strategy development and planning would better posture DoD for an unconventional future. The contemporary environment is inherently complex. It will remain so. The likeliest and most dangerous security challenges emerging from it will be unconventional. "Unconventional," from a DoD perspective, connotes national security conditions and contingencies that are defense-relevant but not necessarily defense-specific. Unconventional security challenges lie substantially outside the realm of traditional warfighting. They are routinely *nonmilitary* in origin and character.[7] Yet, nonmilitary, in this context, does not necessarily mean nonviolent, nonstate, or disordered and unorganized.[8]

This monograph argues that thoughtful evaluation of the most plausible defense-relevant shocks and their deliberate integration into DoD strategy and planning provides senior defense officials with key checks on excessive convention. Further, the institutionalization of deliberate net and risk assessment of defense-relevant shocks, reasoned judgments about their origins, and preliminary analysis of the most appropriate responses to them promises to routinize prudent hedging in DoD strategy and planning. Finally, serial assessment of potential shocks underwrites DoD relevance and resilience in an increasingly unconventional strategic environment. The most recent National Defense

Strategy (NDS) captures this idea when it observes: "The [Department of Defense] should also develop the military capability and capacity to hedge against uncertainty, and the institutional agility and flexibility to plan early and respond effectively alongside interdepartmental, nongovernmental and international partners."[9]

The Department of Defense is doing valuable work on strategic shocks. That work must endure and mature through the upcoming political transition. DoD has initiated an embryonic effort on "strategic trends and shocks."[10] In a critical period of political transition, it might lose momentum with the inevitable change in defense leadership. This would be unfortunate. The new Secretary of Defense and his or her team must continue to build on the work done thus far. Careful examination of the most plausible and disruptive strategic shocks should be routine in all future defense strategy, planning, and decisionmaking.

"KNOWN UNKNOWNS": PREDICTABLE BUT UNPREDICTED STRATEGIC SHOCKS[11]

> (T)here are some risks to national security which . . . can be conceived, but not predicted or fully anticipated. Because they cannot be anticipated, such events are very difficult to plan for effectively. At least two reasons apply. First, by their very nature, these events alter the international system by their reversal of significant trends, thereby undermining the facts upon which future planning is built. Second, many of these events fall outside the scope of traditional or permitted defense planning.
>
> — Sam J. Tangredi[12]

Strategic shocks change the nature of "the game" itself. To Peter Schwartz and Doug Randall, strategic shocks (or "strategic surprises" in their lexicon) are "game changing events."[13] Their occurrence suddenly discredits many or all preexisting assumptions about the environment and those conventions that govern effective navigation through it. Schwartz and Randall conclude:

> Strategic surprises . . . are those . . . events that, if they occur, would make a big difference to the future, force decisionmakers to challenge their own assumptions of how the world works, and require hard choices today.[14]

Schwartz and Randall distinguish strategic shocks or surprises from other contingencies. They argue that they (1) "have an important impact on . . . [the] country"; (2) stretch conventional wisdom in ways that make "it difficult to convince others that the surprise is even possible"; and, finally, (3) are so complex that it is "hard to imagine what can be done in response."[15]

Employing the term "wild card," John L. Peterson defines strategic shocks as those events that have "a direct effect on the human condition"; have "broad, important and sometimes fundamental implications"; and finally, rise and mature "so fast that there is not enough warning to allow the rest of the system to adjust."[16] Thus, game-changing strategic shocks catch national security institutions like DoD by surprise by the speed of their onset, as well as by the breath and depth of their impact. Strategic shocks suddenly and irrevocably change the rules of the game, as well as the contours and composition of playing surface itself.

In a defense context, strategic shocks manifest themselves as sudden surprises to DoD's collective consciousness. They pose grave risks — perhaps even lasting and irreversible harm — to one or more core security interests. Defense-relevant shocks force sudden, unanticipated change in DoD's perceptions about threat, vulnerability, and strategic response. Their unexpected onset forces the whole defense enterprise to rapidly reorient and restructure institutions and employ institutional and operational capabilities in fundamentally different ways, against fundamentally different challenges.

Some of the most plausible defense-relevant strategic shocks remain low probability events. Nonetheless, their impact is so fundamental and consequential that hedging against them is a critical activity for the entire defense enterprise. Again, the post-9/11 period is a clinic in this regard.

Defense-relevant strategic shocks present senior leaders and strategists with complex conceptual challenges. Defense-relevant strategic shocks are thunderbolt events. Absent prior consideration, strategic shocks catch senior defense leaders and strategists flat-footed. They are so strategically dislocating that they cause sudden defense adaptation to new, unfamiliar rule sets or the absence of rules altogether. Defense leaders and strategists are forced by circumstances to make snap judgments on the future efficacy of standing defense paradigms — all under the pressure of time and rapidly changing circumstances. As a consequence, responses to them are vulnerable to having hope and chance versus prudent risk-informed planning as their foundations.

Taking some exception with Tangredi's observation above, they are at once both predictable (and often predicted) but also un- or inadequately anticipated and accounted for.[17] According to a 2007 Naval Postgraduate School (NPS) report, "In hindsight, it is clear that most shocks are the product of long-term trends, and are

6

less disruptive when we have anticipated and responded to [the underlying trends]."[18] In this regard, strategic shocks are less failures in prediction and instead key failures by the strategy and policy community to thoughtfully account for them adequately in strategic planning.

Shocks do, as Tangredi suggests, undermine prevailing strategy and planning assumptions.[19] And thus, they also often lie outside "traditional or permitted" areas of defense inquiry. As a result, they so jar prevailing defense wisdom that they force fundamental changes to some or all long-standing defense priorities. The NPS report observes similarly, "Shocks are disruptive by their very nature and . . . can change how we think about security and the role of the military."[20] Thus, strategic shocks force defense leaders into uncharted operating space. Witness, for example, the unplanned renaissance of CT, COIN, and stability operations within the DoD repertoire.

"Shock" and "surprise" are not necessarily synonymous. Surprise is only half of the equation with respect to defense-relevant shocks. They are distinct from other unexpected strategic contingency events in that they are unanticipated and inadequately accounted for to such an extent that their occurrence triggers fundamental strategic and institutional disruption across the defense enterprise. There is no scientific break point between strategic shock and strategic surprise. The boundary separating the two is a function of an event's strategic impact, the extent of disruption it causes, and the degree to which the defense enterprise anticipated its occurrence in strategy development and planning. High impact contingency events that promise fundamental disruption and occur without the benefit of adequate policy-level anticipation are more likely than not to be strategic shocks (see Figure 1).

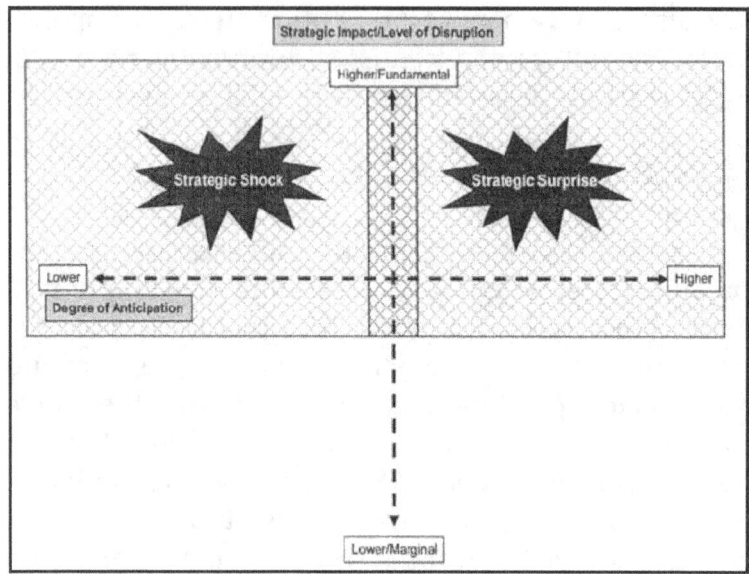

Figure 1. Defense-Relevant Strategic Shock Versus Strategic Surprise.

Saddam Hussein's 1990 invasion of Kuwait was a strategic surprise. It was not a strategic shock. Both the challenge from Iraq's military and the American response to large-scale conventional cross-border incursion were well-considered in both theory and practice. There was no need for a fundamental reorientation of defense strategy and defense priorities in response.

On the other hand, 9/11-like attacks were not necessarily *unpredicted*, but they were nonetheless shocking to the national security establishment. Against a wide universe of compelling defense-relevant challenges, 9/11-like events and the likeliest American response to them were both inadequately considered and undervalued in defense planning. Thus, when they became reality, they proved to be disruptive shocks to the collective defense consciousness. The surprising

8

speed and breadth of change in U.S. perceptions about the threat from terrorism forced an institutional revolution on DoD without the benefit of detailed forethought.

In 1962, Thomas Schelling captured the essence of the defense-relevant strategic shock, in the foreword to Roberta Wohlstetter's classic book *Pearl Harbor: Warning and Decision,* when he observed on the Pearl Harbor attacks:

> The results, at Pearl Harbor, were sudden, concentrated, and dramatic. The failure, however, was cumulative, widespread, and rather drearily familiar . . . (S)urprise is everything involved in a government's . . . failure to anticipate effectively.[21]

There are two routes to defense-relevant shock. Strategic shocks will arrive via one of two distinct paths. The first is rapid, unanticipated arrival at the natural end of a well-recognized and perilous trend line; or, as a corollary, earlier than expected arrival at a dangerous waypoint along that same trend line.[22] Both indicate some substantial and largely unforeseen escalation of recognized hazards. Alternatively, they may arrive via less predictable, discontinuous breaks from trends altogether.[23] These are the rarer "Black Swans."[24] 9/11 might be considered the former. And, although the subject of some debate about its predictability, the sudden collapse of the Soviet Union might fall in the latter category.

This view is consistent with DoD's current perspective on strategic shocks. DoD policymakers define shocks as sudden arrival of exigent conditions "that [punctuate] the evolution of a trend—a discontinuity that either rapidly accelerates [the trend's] pace or significantly changes its trajectory."[25]

The first of these discontinuities implies unanticipated arrival at a way- or endpoint on a recognized trend line. The second reflects sudden onset of the rarer "Black Swan." On the subject of "strategic trends," the most recent defense strategy observes:

> Increasingly, the Department will have to plan for a future security environment shaped by the interaction of powerful strategic trends. These trends suggest a range of plausible futures, some presenting major challenges and security risks.[26]

Shocks emerge from strategic planning territory that Hugh Courtney describes as "Level 3" and "Level 4" uncertainty. Courtney's upper two levels of uncertainty are also consistent with the discussion above. According to Courtney, "Level 3" uncertainty is territory where "(o)ne can identify the range of possible future outcomes, but no obvious point forecast emerges."[27] This range of outcomes is akin to the end- and/or way points on known and dangerous trend lines. "Level 4" uncertainty represents decisionmaking territory where "a limitless range of possible future outcomes" exists.[28] This is the territory of the "Black Swan" — discontinuous breaks in trend lines altogether.

Unconventional, defense-relevant shocks lie in the conceptual territory between the well-considered and the purely speculative. In defense strategy and planning, meaningful consideration of shocks is uncovered, informally-covered, or inadequately-covered ground. Indeed, in spite of nascent work within the Office of the Secretary of Defense (OSD), shocks largely lay in an analytical no man's land separating conventional contingency events from highly incredible or speculative ones. The uncovered ground in between becomes fertile soil for the next shock.

On one side of the no man's land is the well-practiced trade of DoD. It is territory occupied by conventional military competition and now kinetic CT and COIN. Until 9/11, DoD over-subscribed to the first. Since the Iraq War, it hazards over-optimizing for the second.

On the other side of the divide is an incredible or highly speculative extreme that pushes at the far-boundary of defense rationality. Up to a reasonable point, some of this area might still be the target of prudent hedging. However, beyond the point of reason, it becomes a resource consuming distraction. In contemporary defense parlance, this area is exemplified in what the author might call the extreme "disruptive challenge" where the U.S. military might find itself suddenly powerless against the technical advances of a capable state opponent with little or no strategic warning.[29] Figure 2 provides a graphic representation of the two extremes and the analytical no man's land between.

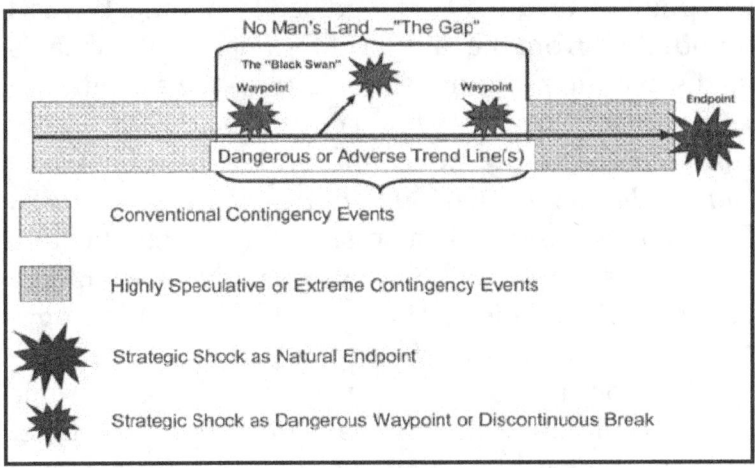

Figure 2. No Man's Land — "The Gap."

9/11 rose from the middle of "no man's land." An illustration is in order here. Prior to 9/11, terrorism was plainly on the defense and national security agenda. There was a clear trend line of increasing terrorist violence and lethality—e.g., 1993 World Trade Center bombings, 1998 East African bombings, the USS *Cole*. "Run-of-the-mill" terrorism was deemed nettlesome but strategically inconsequential. It was "white noise" perpetrated by what some thought to be an unimportant and largely discredited extremist constituency. At the far end of the same spectrum, defense and national security strategists considered nuclear terrorism to be catastrophic, unthinkable, and thus worthy of some defense focus.

There was little meaningful defense consideration of the severity and consequences of terrorism lying on the strategic ground in between. However, in hindsight, one can see that 9/11 marked the U.S. arrival at a natural, dangerous, and underappreciated waypoint on an already recognized trend line. It was a thunderbolt from the middle of the analytical no man's land separating the conventional from the extreme.

The gap between the conventional and well-considered and the incredible or highly speculative should be a priority in future defense analysis. Detailed net and risk assessment between the two extremes is increasingly important to defense strategy and planning. This territory skirts the inside edges of well-considered, defense-relevant, and defense-specific conditions and truly incredible or extreme ones. Admittedly, the boundary demarking the latter is highly subjective. Nonetheless, this middle area has long been undervalued in mainstream defense planning. Here a caution from Thomas Schelling is appropriate. He observes:

The danger is not that we shall read the signals and indicators with too little skill, the danger is in a poverty of expectations — a routine obsession with a few dangers that may be familiar rather than likely.[30]

The gap in the middle is that unconventional ground where irregular, catastrophic, and hybrid "threats of purpose" and "threats of context" rise and mix in complex combinations to challenge core interests.[31] Purposeful threats are defense-specific or defense-relevant security challenges originating in the hostile designs of a consequential opponent. Threats of context are defense-relevant security challenges emerging slowly or suddenly from circumstances endemic to the strategic environment itself; all in the absence of hostile design vis-à-vis the United States.[32]

This middle gap — where threats of purpose and context rise and combine — is the likeliest source of strategic shock for the nation and its defense establishment. Increased focus here may catch the next disruptive surprise early. Thus, it is increasingly important for senior leaders and strategists to examine all plausible waypoints and endpoints along the full length of unfavorable trend lines, as well as credible, discontinuous breaks in the trend lines themselves. Both should be done with a view toward hedging against unforeseen shock. Hugh Courtney is instructive in this regard. He observes:

Scenarios that describe the extreme points in the range of possible outcomes are often relatively easy to develop, but those in between deliver the most information for current strategic decisions and they are the hardest to determine.[33]

13

The most compelling future defense-relevant shocks are likely to be unconventional. Future Secretaries of Defense should recognize that the next defense-relevant shock will likely emerge as a significant surprise to the innately conservative and traditionally-focused DoD establishment. It will be strategically dislocating. It is certain to fall substantially outside established defense convention. And, if left unaccounted for in DoD strategy development and planning, it will vex senior leaders and strategists.

Indeed, the odds are very high against any of the challenges routinely at the top of the traditional defense agenda triggering the next watershed inside DoD. Here it might be valuable to recognize that current defense convention itself may be less a reflection of strategic reality than commonly appreciated.[34] In this regard, the next exigent challenge for DoD is not likely to emerge from deliberate, cross border attack by an aggressive state. Nor, is it likely to arrive via sudden missile attack on an American or allied population. Finally, neither will it likely come from an organized insurgency against a friendly government. These are all now the stock and trade of defense convention, yet probably fail to adequately represent the likeliest defense-specific and defense-relevant realities. Figure 3 below suggests that the contemporary defense reality may already straddle the far extreme of current defense convention, as well as significant uncovered ground in "the gap."

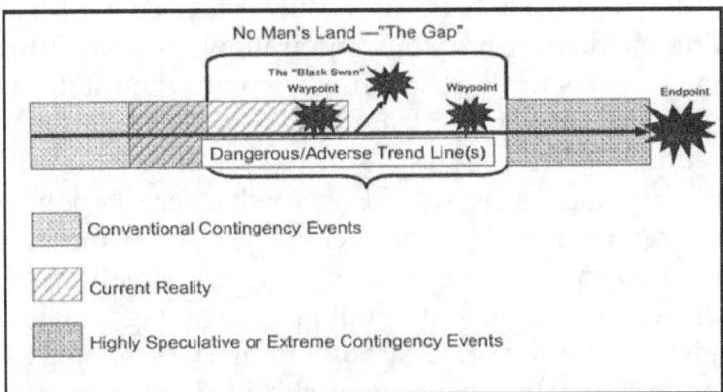

Figure 3. Current Reality May Defy Current Convention.

In this respect, the next compelling defense-relevant threat is likely to appear by purpose and design or accident at the intersection of war of some description,[35] low politics, and chronic instability. It will fall in between the conventional decision and operating space of competing U.S. Government (USG) agencies. It will not lend itself to simple resolution through the traditional application of U.S. instruments of power in their classical combinations. As in the case of both 9/11 and the Iraq insurgency, the next consequential shock for DoD is certain to be unconventional and defense-relevant, not traditional and defense-specific.[36]

Among the most challenging defense-relevant shocks will be those arising in the absence of hostile strategic design.[37] Defense leaders and strategists should be acutely aware that both hostile purpose and strategic context are combining to undermine and threaten core interests. As senior leaders and strategists weigh the hazards of both, they should recognize that looking for the next shock solely in the hostile designs of adversaries is grossly inadequate. Indeed, the strategic environment itself may be the next worst U.S. enemy.

Even shocks born of hostile purpose will look different than current convention allows. Indeed, future purposeful shocks are likeliest to come when state and nonstate competitors learn to effectively circumvent traditional U.S. military overmatch, employing non-military means as war. They will leverage politics, economics, hostile social action, and discriminating nonmilitary violence in innovative combinations. As a result, traditional U.S. military advantages will be sidelined not by breakthrough military technology or concepts, but by the simple absence of a legitimate *casus belli*. These circumstances should be less "shocking," as there is still some latent convention to the prospect of purposeful opponents leveraging nonmilitary innovation as war. Nonetheless, the current defense strategy does recognize the potential for shock in this regard when it observes:

> In some instances, we may not learn that a conflict is underway until it is well-advanced and our options are limited. We must develop better intelligence capabilities to detect, recognize, and analyze new forms of warfare.[38]

The most challenging defense-relevant shocks might emerge from adverse conditions endemic to the environment itself. This is made more certain by the unguided forces of globalization, toxic populism, identity politics, underdevelopment, human/natural disaster, and disease. In the end, shocks emerging from contextual threats might challenge core U.S. interests more fundamentally than any number of prospective purposeful shocks. This is especially true given the degree to which threats of context remain unconsidered or, at a minimum, undervalued in contemporary defense planning and decisionmaking. In the main, threats of context are difficult for the defense establishment to anticipate and combat precisely because:

- There is no single engine or design behind their occurrence;
- They are more out of the proximate control of the United States and its most capable international partners;
- They are much harder to predict and/or track; and finally,
- They are in- or undervulnerable to traditional instruments of U.S. power applied in predictable combinations.

Threats of context might include but are not limited to contagious un- and under-governance; civil violence; the swift catastrophic onset of consequential natural, environmental, and/or human disaster; a rapidly expanding and uncontrolled transregional epidemic; and the sudden crippling instability or collapse of a large and important state. Indeed, pushing at the boundaries of current convention, it would be prudent to add catastrophic dislocation inside the United States or homegrown domestic civil disorder and/or violence to this category as well. The 2008 NDS observes similarly:

> Over the next 20 years physical pressures—population, resource, energy, climatic, and environmental—could combine with rapid social, cultural, technological, and geopolitical change to create greater uncertainty.[39]

Most of these contextual threats are triggers or catalysts. They are the origin of shocks. The extent of the shock is determined by the degree to which any one of these threats is unanticipated or unaccounted for by the strategy and policy community and, as a result, forces revolutionary change on the defense or national security status quo. For example, disruptive civil violence, natural disasters, and epidemics are expected on the near- to mid-term strategic horizon. They will occur around the world. The defense-relevant shock comes when one of these occurs or two or more of these combine in ways that force DoD to fundamentally reorient strategy, capabilities, investments, and concepts in response.

By way of example, realist calculation indicates that epidemics and widespread civil violence might be tolerable in some parts of the world. Shock would result if these occurred inside the United States or inside a key strategic partner to such an extent that they forced DoD to radically re-role for domestic security, population control, consequence management, and stabilization. Likewise, failure of any state is tragic, but not always compelling strategically. However, failure of one or more nuclear states and subsequent nuclear use by competing parties in an intrastate war or nuclear use externally against the United States or a key U.S. ally might force DoD to fundamentally retool for stabilization in a "dirty" environment, and, at the same time, increase its capacity for the armed restoration of responsible control over third party nuclear arsenals.[40]

TRAPPED BY CONVENTION: SEEING THE FUTURE WE WANT?

There is a tendency in our planning to confuse the unfamiliar with the improbable. The contingency we have not considered seriously looks strange; what looks strange is thought improbable; what is improbable need not be considered seriously

— Thomas Schelling[41]

Defense strategy and planning are trapped by excessive convention. DoD has begun to explore strategic shocks in a more thoughtful way. In the past, however, meaningful consideration of strategic shocks was never welcome in mainstream defense strategy and policy development. The past might be prologue in this regard. Until quite recently, meaningful examination of shocks was relegated to the niche worlds of defense futures, concept development, and net assessment. These defense-specific communities, however, limited consideration of shocks to examination of linear or discontinuous changes in the quality of known *military* threats.[42] Until the predictable shock of 9/11, mainstream defense strategists rarely ventured into the territory of unconventional strategic shocks in other than a cursory and speculative manner. In the words of the 9/11 Commission, "Imagination is not a gift usually associated with bureaucracies."[43]

In general, rigorously analyzed strategic shocks were never injected thoughtfully into important pieces of high-level defense guidance—e.g., successive National Military Strategies, Quadrennial Defense Reviews, and biennial Defense Planning Guidance. When strategic shocks or wild cards were mentioned in these, they were often described in overly broad terms and were most often captured in "throw away" language like that from the 1997 National Military Strategy (NMS):

> We can never know with certainty where or when the next conflict will occur, who our next adversary will be, how an enemy will fight, who will join us in a coalition, or precisely what demands will be placed on U.S. forces. A number of "wild card" threats could emerge. . . . Such threats range from the emergence of new technologies . . . to the loss of key allies or alliances and the unexpected overthrow of friendly regimes.[44]

19

Thus, to date, successive Secretaries of Defense have been disinclined to account for shocks in their strategic calculations. There is a predictable and natural sensitivity within the defense establishment against veering too far in the direction of speculation. Likewise, innate military conservatism has consistently forced senior leaders and strategists into the sanctuary of convention. Powerful motivations militate against gambling finite resources or targeting DoD strategy toward worldviews deviating dramatically from established defense norms. Francis Fukuyama suggests this is the product of behaviors bred inside the national security bureaucracy. He observes:

> Those who deal professionally with global politics, foreign policy, and national security affairs have particular biases when it comes to thinking about the future. Their biases generate a perceptual incentive structure that throws off their general capacity for accurate prediction.[45]

Summarizing the arguments presented in his recent edited volume on strategic shocks and wild cards, Fukuyama concludes that failures of cognition, resources, and institutional weaknesses all contribute to the widespread tendency to leave strategic shocks out of deliberate strategic planning.[46] On the issue of "human cognition," he decries the dangers resident in "shared mental models" that result in group think. He observes more generally, "(L)eaders have a hard time discounting the present value of events that will take place in the future."[47]

With respect to resources, he argues, "Even if individuals . . . are cognitively prepared for a future contingency, they often do not have the right incentives to hedge against it properly." He continues, "Hedging is costly, and no organization can possibly hedge against all possible contingencies."[48] Finally, on the issue of institutions, Fukuyama suggests, "Hedging against future risks . . . also requires collective action, specifically a sharing of decisionmaking authority and a pooling of resources across organizational and international boundaries."[49] The implication is that the capacity for shared responsibility and collective action are rare qualities inside the U.S. national security and defense establishments.

DoD's prevailing, pre-9/11 "mental model" biased it in the direction of excessive convention. All of the aforementioned were evidenced in the behaviors of pre-9/11 DoD. The mental model operative in DoD prior to 9/11 rested on the 60 (plus)-year-old theology of industrial and information-age military conflict. The role of DoD was to "fight and win wars." "Wars" by definition were limited to the formal clash of arms between the United States and hostile state competitors. Defense strategy and planning were driven by linear extrapolations of existing or perceived sources of future military conflict—resurgent Russia, rising China, recalcitrant Iraq, miscalculating North Korea. There would be future security challenges. The only difference between the Cold War and the post-Cold War epoch was quantity—cumulatively more consequential challengers; and quality—a universe of threats that were dangerous but not so existentially.

In this mental frame, the only threats of consequence were states; specifically, state militaries. Among these, the sources of strategic shock were thought to be those that might have the potential for sudden unanticipated acquisition and employment of new, more threatening ("disruptive") military capabilities or designs. There would, for example, be an immediate regional challenge from a small universe of second-rate military powers prone to miscalculation. And, on the mid- to long-term horizon, emergence of near-peer or peer military competitor was accepted as gospel.

The fear was that one or more of these state competitors would acquire "revolutionary technology" and undertake "associated military innovation" that would "fundamentally alter long-established concepts of warfare" and undermine traditional U.S. dominance.[50] The likeliest future candidates at the high end of this category were a more activist and bellicose China or, more distantly, a reenergized and newly capable Russian Federation.[51]

Issues having little to do with organized military competition between states were considered boutique, speculative, and distracting from the real business of defense planning and traditional warfighting. This narrative stuck in the U.S. defense community precisely because it conformed to mental models shared by most inside DoD. 9/11 and subsequent experience in Iraq, Afghanistan, and the wider war on terrorism (WoT) changed all prevailing "mental models." However, the extent to which it did so in a durable way is an open question. The defense and military bias in favor of convention is likely more deeply entrenched than outside observers appreciate.

Earlier and more detailed examination of the gap might have limited the intensity of the post-9/11 shock. Until 9/11 and subsequent irregular wars in Iraq and Afghanistan, defense strategists were the virtual prisoners of mechanical planning and programming processes from the theater- to the national-strategic level. These lent themselves easily to the evaluation of well-structured adversary military forces and actions. Predictably, they also resulted in the perpetuation of Cold War-like defense planning scenarios, stock war plans, force sizing and planning constructs, and acquisition strategies that:

- First, were conceived of according to classically realist convention and inherited from or derivatives of strategic concepts and constructs more appropriate to the Cold War;
- Second, were often mistaken for or masquerading as coherent defense strategy;
- Third, failed to account for dangerous forces of social and political insecurity spinning off the decomposing Cold War order;
- Fourth, reflected a security environment senior leaders and strategists were intellectually best prepared for and also most comfortable with; and,[52]
- Fifth, ultimately proved unresponsive to a new, more unconventional defense-relevant challenge set.

Hindsight argues that defense concepts, sizing and shaping constructs, and plans devised in the decade prior to 9/11 were wholly inappropriate to the environment likeliest to emerge from the shock of the Cold War's collapse.[53] For example, neither successive force sizing and shaping constructs nor a whole range of associated U.S. war plans would have survived rigorous analysis intact were they measured against the serial human, material, and fiscal demands of simultaneous COIN/Security, Stabilization, and Reconstruction Operations (SSTRO) campaigns in Iraq and Afghanistan, or the persistent and unceasing demands of a wider WoT. A more thoughtful and unbiased analysis of the near- to long-term national security horizon in the wake of the Cold War might have resulted in a clearer, more nuanced, and more realistic view of defense-relevant demands in the 21st century.

However, this more thoughtful and unbiased analysis also would have required senior defense leaders and strategists to explore the gap between conventional contingencies and extreme or speculative contingencies in much greater detail. Had this analysis occurred, it might have identified the increasing U.S. vulnerability to a whole range of consequential and potentially shocking challenges that were more complex and more unconventional than those imagined by defense leaders and strategists who continued to operate under a discredited Cold War rule set. Indeed, it may have accounted for the increasing likelihood of successive post-Cold War shocks to the defense establishment—e.g., 9/11, the WoT, and the Iraq insurgency—and the attendant requirement for DoD to either adjust to or be overwhelmed by the demands of the contemporary environment.

Thoughtful assessments like this also would have put a number of contemporary (and preferred) defense priorities and methods at substantial risk. This would run afoul with a range of bureaucratic interests inside the Pentagon. Traditional core competencies, long-lead weapons programs and investments, concepts of operation, and budget share would all have been in jeopardy to one extent or another. In some form, these inherently bureaucratic obstacles remain extant today.

9/11 was important. However, was it important enough to make DoD's appreciation of unconventional shocks irreversible? Without question, 9/11 was a "game changer" for DoD.[54] So, too, was the sudden onset of the insurgency in Iraq. In the wake of 9/11, the on-going WoT, and active irregular conflicts in Iraq and Afghanistan, senior DoD leaders and strategists increasingly recognize the importance of defense-relevant shocks. On-going efforts like DoD's "strategic trends and shocks" initiative and the State Department's "Project Horizon" are embryonic efforts intended in part to institutionalize the concept of strategic shock in routine government planning and decisionmaking.[55]

Both efforts are futures oriented and preventive. Both are intended to help define near-term choices and decision space. Finally, both seek to shape priorities, capabilities, and strategic design in ways that will posture the defense and national security establishments to better anticipate, prevent, and, if prevention fails, respond decisively to sudden strategic shock in the future.

The extent to which the national security establishment appreciates the potential value associated with maturing either or both of these efforts is uncertain. Yet, if the previous 7 years is an indication of a new more unconventional national security status quo, both "strategic trends and shocks" and "Project Horizon" merit continued support and development. The current defense team acknowledges this imperative. For example, on the subject of strategic trends and the prospect for their triggering dislocating shocks, the 2008 NDS concludes, "How [strategic trends] interact and the nature of the shocks they might generate is uncertain; the fact that they will influence the future security environment is not."[56]

SEEING THE WHOLE FUTURE: INCORPORATING SHOCKS IN DEFENSE STRATEGY

Without sophisticated advanced consideration of unconventional strategic shocks specifically, DoD's frame of reference and tool-kit will be inadequate to contend with the most dangerous and complex future contingencies. Anticipation of unconventional shocks in particular is exceedingly important. This calls for a disciplined approach to their deliberate identification and analysis.

In this regard, it is difficult to find something one is not first committed to looking for. The degree of danger or harm from defense-relevant strategic shocks more broadly is directly proportionate to DoD's ability to see them coming in sufficient time and with sufficient clarity to affect meaningful advanced preparation. This requires a commitment to look for and examine shocks in the first place.

Once identified as plausible, the most disruptive prospective shocks must become the subject of detailed interdisciplinary examination. All of this argues for continued defense and interagency investment in and routinization of initiatives like "strategic trends and shocks" and "Project Horizon." The current defense team is inclined in this direction. According the recent NPS report:

> One of the key objectives of the (d)epartment is developing a systematic process and intellectual foundation to identify key trends and shocks, and subsequent impacts of these shocks.[57]

Identifying on-coming defense-relevant shocks will never be a DoD responsibility alone. The more unconventional the prospective shock, the more this is the case. Likewise, preventing shocks or responding to them will always require the innovative blending of all instruments of national power. Both advanced warning of impending shock and the decisive blending of defense and non-defense resources in response rely on a whole-of-government commitment to tackle the topic from its infancy in an intellectually disciplined fashion. Having already invested in preliminary consideration of strategic shocks, DoD's ongoing efforts should continue and mature in this regard.

This intellectual heavy-lifting requires that shocks benefit from sufficient emphasis in future defense strategy development. This demands the interest and engagement of high-level DoD leadership. It further requires defense strategists who are adequately socialized to look for and contend with critical uncertainties, indications of sudden change in the environment, and, finally, shock. In general, it requires a defense establishment that is predisposed toward curiosity about and investigation into the unconventional and the unknown. All of these are in some respects countercultural.

In short, strategic shocks should increasingly enter defense convention as a key driver for strategy development and strategic planning. According to Schwartz and Randall, "One cannot foresee strategic surprises without being imaginative, but the results will not be believed without being systematic." [58] Indeed, if 9/11, the WoT, and the Iraq insurgency are indicators, deliberate consideration within DoD of some key prospective shocks will be more important to strategic decisionmaking than will detailed examination of other long-standing conventional policy drivers. The latter are consistently over-considered and thus, well-understood. The recent past provides a tragic example of the "failure of imagination" in this respect.

Naturally, there are both benefits and hazards to incorporating strategic shocks more broadly into defense decisionmaking. However, the benefits outweigh the hazards. According to Tangredi:

> Assessing the potential effects of wildcards may bring one to the point where imagination overtakes research. Nevertheless, sketching the outlines and prospective impacts of such unanticipated events helps identify the alternatives against which hedging strategies may be appropriate.[59]

As suggested above, deliberate consideration of the most consequential, high-impact unconventional shocks must be an interdisciplinary effort occurring at the intersection of strategy and policy development, intelligence, and defense analysis. Synthesized, interdisciplinary judgments on shocks ensures that any process chartered to examine them avoids the trap of becoming an unfocused, speculative, and overly academic examination of "what if" and instead becomes a policy-relevant input into the Secretary of Defense's decision space on the merits of plausibility, strategic relevance, and impact. In order for these interdisciplinary judgments to have requisite influence on higher-level DoD decisionmaking, any examination of shocks must occur in close proximity to and have the attention of the Secretary of Defense himself.

ROUTINIZING IMAGINATION: PLAUSIBLE UNCONVENTIONAL SHOCKS

Illustrations of prospective shocks are more compelling to policymakers than are generalized descriptions of dangerous trends. General descriptions of dangerous trends, while important contextually, are not nearly as powerful to policymakers as are tight, illustrative descriptions of the most dangerous endpoints, waypoints, or discontinuous breaks in trend lines. Paraphrasing the 9/11 Commission, it is critically important for DoD to "routinize" consideration of plausible strategic shocks so as to posture it to better anticipate, hedge against, and respond to them in the most effective and risk-informed way.[60] *The following unconventional shocks are illustrative.*[61] They are only intended to demonstrate the type of disruptive shock groups that merit deliberate consideration in future defense strategy deliberations.

Strategic State Collapse.[62]

In the international system, some states matter more than others. There are a number of states whose stable functioning is uniquely important to the United States and its interests. Most of these states harbor vast potential for harm should they succumb to sudden, catastrophic instability or failure. This is true regardless of their pre-collapse disposition toward the United States—friendly, benign, or neutral. These are "strategic states" that:

- Possess significant employable weapons of mass destruction (WMD) capacity;[63]
- Possess significant strategic resources, economic capacity, and/or dominant geographic leverage;
- Are in close proximity to the United States or a key strategic partner and have a large dependent population vulnerable to uncontrolled migration;
- Could with unanticipated destabilization trigger contagious instability in an important region; and/or,
- Are allies or key strategic partners.

None of these categories are mutually exclusive. Failure, uncontrolled instability, or collapse of states exhibiting one or more of these qualities would present the United States with complex hybrid challenges. They may, for example, pose grave harm to the security of an important region. Alternatively, they may suddenly provide consequential opponents of the United States unrestricted access to or influence over a victim state's assets, resources, and political outcomes.

There are a number of plausible collapse scenarios. Triggers for collapse are rooted in irregular, catastrophic, and hybrid threats of purpose and context. Given the recognized instability of some strategic states, collapse might mark a natural endpoint to an already recognized and unfavorable trend. In other cases, strategic state collapse may arrive via "Black Swan" with little or no strategic warning. For DoD, the collapsed strategic state presents an immensely complex defense relevant challenge. Sheer capacity alone indicates a decisive DoD role in restoring a new more stable status quo.

Fulfilling that role would be problematic given the character of the post-collapse environment.[64] In the collapsed strategic state, elements of the armed forces and security services may remain under coherent command and control and actively resist intervention. Dedicated agents of the prior unstable status quo are prone to fight—often violently—to protect or restore vestiges of the old order. Criminals and "pop-up militias" are likely to carve out new, defensible spheres of influence from pieces of the fallen state. Adjacent powers will rush in physically, politically, and/or materially to decisively influence outcomes. Long-repressed political constituencies will be prone to seek out former oppressors and exact vengeance. Local nationalists will resist foreign imposed or inspired solutions. Some internal constituencies will fight to rebalance political authority. Others will fight against that rebalancing. Finally, supercharged indigenous and expatriate constituencies may sow instability beyond the borders of the victim state. All of this will occur in an environment where the surety of nuclear or biological weapons is in question, critical strategic resources are at risk, and/or the core interests of adjacent states are threatened by spillover. Further still, this will all occur in a sea of abject human insecurity.

One of the most dangerous prospective contingencies in this regard might be collapse of a large capable state that results in a nuclear civil war. Uncontrolled proliferation in the event of a nuclear state's collapse is an ever-present threat. However, here also DoD would have to contend with stabilization in the aftermath of nuclear use. It might be the lead agent in reassertion of responsible control over substantial nuclear weapons capabilities. Finally, it would likely be responsible for the armed separation of nuclear-armed opponents and the deliberate disarmament of the various parties to the conflict. All of this would occur under the constant threat of continued nuclear use within or outside the confines of the victim state.

Violent, Strategic Dislocation Inside the United States.

As a community, the defense establishment swears to protect and defend the constitution against all enemies foreign and domestic. DoD's role in combating "domestic enemies" has never been thoughtfully examined. Thus, there is perhaps no greater source of strategic shock for DoD than operationalizing that component of the oath of service in a widespread domestic emergency that entails rapid dissolution of public order in all or significant parts of the United States.

While likely not an immediate prospect, this is clearly a "Black Swan" that merits some visibility inside DoD and the Department of Homeland Security. To the extent events like this involve organized violence against local, state, and national authorities and exceed the capacity of the former two to restore public order and protect vulnerable populations, DoD would be required to fill the gap. This is largely uncharted strategic territory.

Widespread civil violence inside the United States would force the defense establishment to reorient priorities in extremis to defend basic domestic order and human security. Deliberate employment of weapons of mass destruction or other catastrophic capabilities, unforeseen economic collapse, loss of functioning political and legal order, purposeful domestic resistance or insurgency, pervasive public health emergencies, and catastrophic natural and human disasters are all paths to disruptive domestic shock.

An American government and defense establishment lulled into complacency by a long-secure domestic order would be forced to rapidly divest some or most external security commitments in order to address rapidly expanding human insecurity at home. Already predisposed to defer to the primacy of civilian authorities in instances of domestic security and divest all but the most extreme demands in areas like civil support and consequence management, DoD might be forced by circumstances to put its broad resources at the disposal of civil authorities to contain and reverse violent threats to domestic tranquility. Under the most extreme circumstances, this might include use of military force against hostile groups inside the United States. Further, DoD would be, by necessity, an essential enabling hub for the continuity of political authority in a multi-state or nationwide civil conflict or disturbance.

A whole host of long-standing defense conventions would be severely tested. Under these conditions and at their most violent extreme, civilian authorities, on advice of the defense establishment, would need to rapidly determine the parameters defining the legitimate use of military force inside the United States. Further still, the whole concept of conflict termination and/or transition to the primacy of civilian security institutions would be uncharted ground. DoD is already challenged by stabilization abroad. Imagine the challenges associated with doing so on a massive scale at home.

Politics, Economics, Social Action, and Political Violence as Hybrid War.

The United States might also consider the prospect that hostile state and/or nonstate actors might individually or in concert combine hybrid methods effectively to resist U.S. influence in a nonmilitary manner.[65] This is clearly an emerging trend. Imagine, for example, a China-Russia axis that collectively employs substantial political power within international institutions and markets to hold key American interests at risk. At the international level, actors like this might employ extant and emerging political/economic arrangements as instruments for purposeful resistance and war.[66]

At the national and subnational level, purposeful opponents could synchronize nonmilitary effort, agitating quasi-legitimate proxies into concerted social action and precision political violence targeted at nullifying traditional U.S. military advantages, limiting American freedom of action, and adversely shaping the strategic choices of or political outcomes inside key but vulnerable American partners.[67] Imagine "a new era of containment with the United States as the nation to be contained" where the principal tools and methods of war involve everything but those associated with traditional military conflict.[68] Imagine that the sources of this "new era of containment" are widespread; predicated on nonmilitary forms of political, economic, and violent action; in the main, sustainable over time; and finally, largely invulnerable to effective reversal through traditional U.S. advantages.

The pressure on the United States would be cumulative and persistent. In the extreme, it could drive U.S. decisionmakers into increasingly desperate and potentially illegitimate counteraction. Under these circumstances, when competitor militaries are in the mix, they are less tools focused directly against U.S. military superiority and more effective foils against American military intimidation. In this regard, U.S. military forces would be sidelined. Employment of U.S. military power would hold little promise for reversing adverse political and economic conditions. Further, the overt use of military force by the United States would largely be viewed as illegitimate for redress of competitor success in nonmilitary domains. Finally, should the competition involve major competitors like China or Russia, U.S. military action might hazard unacceptable costs or unwanted and uncontrolled escalation.[69]

In this regard, the role of DoD would be more nuanced but also critical. This is particularly true to the extent that a hybrid competitor leverages some discriminate political violence against the United States or its partners as a force multiplier. Under conditions of hybrid war fought largely with nonmilitary and often nonviolent means, defense capabilities for direct action and intelligence gathering would need to be fine-tuned to both the more unconventional character of the conflict, as well as the high risks associated with military imprecision and miscalculation.

To the extent a hybrid conflict like this endures and remains substantially nonmilitary in character, DoD might witness both a significant re-rolling and a substantial loss of material resources as U.S. political leaders shore up more useful nonmilitary instruments of power. In either case, there is no contemporary strategic or doctrinal appreciation for the role of DoD in warfare prosecuted against the United States by other than military and predominantly nonviolent ways and means. Strategic shock would follow.

CONCLUSION — AVOIDING THE NEXT BLUE RIBBON PANEL — OR WORSE

The aforementioned are admittedly extreme. They are not, however, implausible or fantastical. Avoiding the next "blue ribbon panel," chartered to investigate future failures of strategic imagination, requires that DoD continue its commitment to identifying and analyzing the most credible unconventional shocks on the strategic horizon. Increased attention to unconventional shocks in defense strategy should neither supplant prudent hedging against conventional surprise nor routine preparation for the likeliest defense-specific traditional, irregular, and catastrophic challenges. It should, however, become increasingly important in routine defense decisionmaking.

Historically, shocks like Pearl Harbor, 9/11, and the Iraq insurgency have generated wrenching periods of self-examination. However, these periods of introspection most often focus on solving the last problem versus deliberately avoiding or contending with the next one. For example, DoD is admittedly better at COIN and CT in light of its post-9/11 experience. It is, however, reasonable to ask how relevant these are corporately to the next defense-relevant strategic shock. Absent continued reconnaissance into the future, there is no good answer to this question.

Thus, prudent net and risk assessment of (1) the myriad waypoints along dangerous trend lines; (2) the sudden or unanticipated arrival at the end of the same trends; and finally, (3) rapid onset of the rarer "Black Swan" are increasingly important to DoD. Under this administration, valuable work has begun in this regard. This work should continue to mature uninterrupted. Preemptive examination of the most plausible "known unknowns" represents a reasoned down payment on strategic preparedness and an essential defense investment in strategic hedging against an uncertain and dangerous future.

It would be wise for the next defense team to recall the experience of its predecessors. On September 11th, 2001, the latter witnessed the disruptive collision of defense convention and strategic reality. The rest, as they say, is history.

ENDNOTES

1. Hart Seely, "The Poetry of Donald Rumsfeld: Recent Work by the Secretary of Defense," *Slate*, available from *www.slate.com/ id/2081042/*, accessed August 28, 2008. Seely quotes Secretary of Defense Donald Rumsfeld's now famous assertion, "As we know, there are known knowns. There are things we know we know. We also know there are *known unknowns*. That is to say, we know there are some things we do not know. But there are also unknown unknowns. The ones we don't know we don't know."

2. This is a common theme in post-9/11 government and academic commentary. See, for example, *National Commission on Terrorist Attacks Upon the Nation, The 9/11 Commission Report*, available from *cnn.net/cnn/US/resources/9.11.report/911Report.pdf*, accessed December 27, 2007, pp. 339-348; and Michael Ignatieff, "The Burden," *New York Times Magazine*, January 5, 2003, available from *www.faculty.washington.edu/msingh/ignatieff.htm*. The 9/11 Commission argued that first among the four critical failures that led to 9/11 or, at a minimum, led to the United States being caught unaware by 9/11 was a failure of "imagination." Similarly, Ignatieff observed, "It was also, in the 1990s, a general failure of historical imagination, an inability of the post-cold war West to grasp that the emerging crisis of state order in so many overlapping zones of the world . . . would eventually become a security threat at home."

3. Jack Davis, *Improving CIA Analytic Performance: Strategic Warning*, Kent Center Occasional Papers, available from *www. cia.gov/library/kent-center-occaissional-papers/vol1no1.htm*, accessed December 6, 2007.

4. See Peter Schwartz, *Inevitable Surprises: Thinking Ahead in a Time of Turbulence*, New York: Gotham Books, 2003, p. ix; Francis Fukuyama, "Chapter 1: The Challenges of Uncertainty: An Introduction," in Francis Fukuyama, ed., *Blindside: How to Anticipate Forcing Events and Wild Cards in Global Politics, An American Interest Book*, Washington DC: Brookings Institution Press, 2007, p. 1; and Francis Fukuyama, "Chapter 15: Afterward," in *ibid.*, p. 170. Both Fukuyama and Schwartz suggest that 9/11 and the Iraq insurgency were "strategic shocks."

5. Both the terms *defense-relevant* and *defense-specific* are used in this monograph. *Defense-relevant* security challenges or conditions are mostly nonmilitary in character but should be of substantial interest to DoD. A *defense-specific* challenge is one that springs from a military source and requires primary involvement by DoD.

6. This point was raised in a conversation on this paper by Dr. Carl Van Dyke, a Senior National Intelligence Officer with the National Intelligence Council's Office of the National Intelligence Officer for Long Range Warning.

7. In this regard, military connotes those threats, activities, capabilities, or circumstances associated with the armed forces of states. Nonmilitary connotes security challenges, activities, capabilities, or circumstances whose origin and form have little in common with conventional conceptions of state armed forces.

8. The same points are argued in the forthcoming CSIS publication by the author entitled "Shifting Emphasis: Leaders, Strategists, and Operators in an Era of Persistent Unconventional Conflict."

9. Department of Defense (DoD), *National Defense Strategy*, June 2008, p. 5.

10. The "Strategic Trends and Shocks" project on-going within OSD Policy Planning is a preliminary venture into the routinized inclusion of strategic shocks in defense strategy development. For helpful descriptions of this effort, see Naval Postgraduate School (NPS) Transformation Chair, Forces Transformation Chairs Meeting: Visions of Transformation 2025—Shocks and Trends, February 21, 2007, available from *www.tfxchairs.net/cms/ files/TFX%20Mtg%20FEB07%20Report.doc*, accessed August 21, 2008; Terry Pudas, *Trends and Shocks: An Alternative Construct for Defense Planning*, available from *www.federaltimes.com/index. php?S=2752923*, accessed May 19, 2007; and DoD, June 2008, pp. 4-5.

11. See Schwartz, p. xvii. Schwartz argues that shock (or in his words surprise) is inevitable and predictable. He concludes the preface with the following, "History provides ample reason to believe that we can expect inevitable surprises ahead."

12. Sam J. Tangredi, "Chapter Seven, Wild Cards," McNair Paper 63: *All Possible Wars? Toward a Consensus View of the Future Security Environment, 2001-2025,* November 2000, available from *www.ndu.edu/inss/McNair/mcnair63/63_07.htm,* accessed May 19, 2008.

13. Peter Schwartz and Doug Randall, "Chapter 9, Ahead of the Curve: Anticipating Strategic Surprise," in Fukuyama, ed., *Blindside,* p. 93.

14. *Ibid.,* p. 93.

15. *Ibid.,* p. 94.

16. John L. Peterson, *Out of the Blue: Wild Cards and Other Big Future Surprises; How to Anticipate and Respond to Profound Change,* Washington, DC: The Arlington Institute, 1997, p. 10.

17. See Schwartz, 2003, p. 3. Schwartz observes:

There are many things we can rely on, but three of them are most critical to keep in mind in any turbulent environment.

First: There will be more surprises.

Second: We will be able to deal with them.

Third: We can anticipate many of them. In fact we can make some pretty good assumptions about how most of them will play out.

We can't know the consequences in advance . . . but we know many of the surprises to come. Even the most devastating surprises . . . are often predictable because they have their roots in the driving forces at work today.

18. NPS Transformation Chair, p. 3.

19. *Ibid.* This is consistent with the DoD view of strategic shocks. The 2007 Naval Postgraduate School report suggests that DoD's official view is that strategic shocks "undermine the assumptions on which all current policies are based."

20. *Ibid.*

21. Thomas Schelling, "Foreword," in Roberta Wohlstetter, *Pearl Harbor: Warning and Decision*, Stanford, CA: Stanford University Press, 1962, p. viii.

22. For a valuable description of the idea of "trend lines" in a DoD context, see Naval Postgraduate School Transformation Chair, p. 3. Here trends are described as "(a) path along which events tend to evolve predictably."

23. These two conclusions were the product of an informal discussion between the author and Kathleen Hicks of the Center for Strategic and International Studies and Robert Scher of the consulting firm Booze-Allen-Hamilton.

24. See Nassim Nicholas Taleb, *The Black Swan: The Impact of the Highly Improbable*, New York: Random House, 2007. Taleb argues a "Black Swan" has "three attributes." First, they "lie outside the realm of regular expectations"; second, they promise "an extreme impact"; and, third, "in spite of its outlier status, human nature makes us concoct explanations for its occurrence after the fact, making it explainable and predictable."

25. NPS Transformation Chair, p. 3.

26. DoD, June 2008, p. 4.

27. Hugh Courtney, *20/20 Foresight: Crafting Strategy in an Uncertain World*, Boston: Harvard Business School Press, 2001, p. 29.

28. *Ibid.*, p. 32.

29. See DoD, *The National Defense Strategy of the United States of America*, March 2005, p. 3. The 2005 National Defense Strategy defines "disruptive challenges" as those that "come from

adversaries who develop and use break-through technologies to negate current U.S. advantages in key operational domains."

30. Schelling, p. viii.

31. The author described irregular, catastrophic and hybrid challenges in great detail in a previous monograph. See Nathan Freier, *Strategic Competition and Resistance in the 21st Century: Traditional, Irregular, Catastrophic, and Hybrid Challenges in Context*, May 2007, available from *www.strategicstudiesinstitute.army.mil/pdffiles/pub782.pdf*, accessed August 5, 2008. The author discusses threats of purpose and context in detail in the forthcoming CSIS monograph "Shifting Emphasis: Leaders, Strategists, and Operators in an Era of Persistent Unconventional Conflict." On what the author means by the term "core interests," see Peter Bergen and Laurie Garrett, "Report of the Working Group on State Security and Transnational Threats," The Princeton Project on National Security, available from *www.wws.princeton.edu/ppns/conferences/reports/fall/SSTT.pdf*, accessed December 27, 2007. The Princeton working group led by Bergen and Garrett identified a construct of "six fundamental interests" useful to consider as a template. These include "economic prosperity; governance continuity; ideological sustainability; military capability; population well-being; and territorial integrity."

32. See Phil Williams, *From the New Middle Ages to a New Dark Age: The Decline of the State and U.S. Strategy*, Carlisle, PA: Strategic Studies Institute, U.S. Army War College, June 2008, available from *www.Strategic StudiesInstitute.army.mil/*, accessed September 11, 2008. Williams reinforces this point when he observes,

> In the 21st century in most parts of the world, issues of security and stability have little to do with traditional power politics, military conflict between states, and issues of grand strategy. Instead, they revolve around the disruptive consequences of globalization, governance, public safety, inequality, urbanization, violent nonstate actors, and the like.

Later, Williams returns to this point when he says,

In a sense, states are being overwhelmed by complexity, fragmentation, and demands they simply are unable to meet. They are experiencing an unsettling diminution in their capacity to manage political, social, and economic problems that are increasingly interconnected, intractable, and volatile.

33. Courtney, *20/20 Foresight*, pp. 125-126.

34. Dr. Phil Williams, a Visiting Research Professor at the U.S. Army's Strategic Studies Institute, made this observation during a conversation on a draft version of this monograph.

35. See war. (n.d.), *Dictionary.com Unabridged* (v 1.1), available from *dictionary.reference.com/browse/war*, accessed August 5, 2008. Here war should be considered "active hostility or contention; conflict; contest."

36. See DoD, March 2005, p. 2. The word "traditional" in this context implies "challenges posed by states employing recognized military capabilities and forces in well-understood forms of military competition and conflict."

37. The following section includes adaptations of arguments made by the author in the forthcoming CSIS monograph "Shifting Emphasis: Leaders, Strategists, and Operators in an Era of Persistent Unconventional Conflict."

38. DoD, June 2008, p. 4.

39. *Ibid.*

40. *Ibid.*, p. 9.

41. Schelling, p. vii.

42. *Military* is this regard connotes security challenges, activities, capabilities, or circumstances associated with the armed forces of states.

43. *National Commission on Terrorist Attacks Upon the Nation, The 9/11 Commission Report*, available from *cnn.net/cnn/US/*

resources/9.11.report/911Report.pdf, accessed December 27, 2007, p. 344.

44. DoD, "Section III: Defense Strategy," *Quadrennial Defense Review*, May 1997, available from *accessedwww.fas.org/man/docs/qdr/sec3.html*, accessed May 19, 2008.

45. Fukuyama, "Chapter 1," in Fukuyama, ed., *Blindside*, p. 2.

46. Fukuyama, "Chapter 15," in *ibid.*, pp. 169-172.

47. *Ibid.*, pp. 169-170.

48. *Ibid.*, p. 171.

49. *Ibid.*

50. DoD, March 2005, p. 3.

51. See DoD, June 2008, pp. 10-11. This trend endures today. Note the language in the current NDS.

52. See DoD, March 2005, p. iii. The 2005 NDS recognizes this latter point when, in the foreword, Secretary Rumsfeld observes, "The National Defense Strategy outlines our approach to dealing with challenges we will likely confront, not just those we are currently best prepared to meet."

53. *Ibid.*, pp. 2-3.

54. See, for example, Schwartz and Randall, p. 93. With respect to 9/11, Schwartz and Randall observe, "(E)ven the most devastating surprises are often inevitable. Many people did anticipate the terrorist attacks of September 11 . . . Yet, most Americans, as well as officials in both the Clinton and Bush administrations, focused their attention elsewhere while the inevitable grew imminent."

55. For a discussion of "Project Horizon," see Sid Kaplan, *Project Horizon – A New Approach to Interagency Planning*, available from *www.epa.gov/osp/futures/Project Horizon.pdf*, accessed May 19, 2008.

56. Department of Defense, 2008, p. 5.

57. NPS Transformation Chair, p. 3.

58. Schwartz and Randall, p. 97-98.

59. Tangredi, "Chapter Seven: Wild Cards."

60. *National Commission on Terrorist Attacks Upon the Nation, The 9/11 Commission Report*, p. 344.

61. The detail expressed herein does not reflect official U.S. government policy.

62. See DoD, 2008, p. 9; and NPS Transformation Chair, p. 6. Strategic state collapse is clearly on the defense radar screen as a prospective strategic shock. The author is currently writing a monograph on the policy implications associated with strategic state collapse.

63. The author is principally concerned here with sizeable nuclear or biological capabilities.

64. See Freier, *Strategic Competition*, p. 58-59. A similar description of strategic state collapse is included in a previous monograph by the author.

65. *Ibid.*, pp. 47-52.

66. In an initial conversation on this project with with D. Burgess Laird of the Institute for Defense Analysis, Laird raised existing institutions like the Shanghai Cooperation Council, the United Nations General Assembly, etc. as potential forums for future coordinated political competition with the United States.

67. *Ibid.*, pp. 48-49.

68. Schwartz and Randall, p. 108.

69. Freier, *Stategic Competition*, p. 51.